COPERNICUS

COPERNICUS

SHORT STORIES

JOSHUA FIELDS

To order additional copies of this book, contact:
Xlibris Corporation
1-888-795-4274
www.Xlibris.com
Orders@Xlibris.com
111140

CONTENTS

Holy Maria...9

Jane vs. John...20

In The Name of the Father.................................28

The Lottery...35

Iron and Wine..44

Regardless of Time, Season, or Human Conduct—

the face of the Earth is warmed everyday

Jeffrey Allen

HOLY MARIA

April, 2006
Oaxaca, Mexico

Elina was in the kitchen fixing breakfast for her family. Her husband, Esteban, was a high school history teacher. Her boys (Fidel, Emillo, and Jose) were also getting ready to attend school that morning. Fidel, the oldest boy, was giving his younger siblings orders to stop wasting time and get dressed.

Esteban was the first to attend the table. Elina, pleased, brought him his morning coffee. "Looks like a nice day today," she said.

"Not as long as Ortiz is still in office," he responded.

Elina smiled, "Don't worry about Ortiz. Think of your boys."

"My boys are directly impacted by Ortiz. We must fight."

"Fight if you must, Esteban, but first eat your breakfast."

Fidel, Emillo, and Jose pushed their way onto the scene. "Boys, stop fighting," said Elina.

"Dad," said Fidel. "Do you think there will be a protest today?"

"Not today son," said Esteban. "But, a movement is underway."

Elina then interrupted, "I don't want to hear any more of movements or protests. I just want to enjoy breakfast with my family."

Esteban grinned and told the boys to listen to their mother.

June, 2006

The strike began in protest of low wages and the call for Ortiz to resign as state governor. Three thousand police were sent in to disrupt the assembly. Many protesters were left hospitalized. Ortiz remained steadfast in his determination to maintain control. Esteban joined the Popular Assembly of the Peoples of Oaxaca. The group soon took over the city in open rebellions.

August, 2006

"Dad," said Fidel. "Did you really take over the radio station?"

"I did my part," said Esteban. "Now, go get cleaned up for dinner."

Esteban then joined Elina in the kitchen. "What's for dinner tonight?" he asked.

"Your favorite," said Elina. "Empanadas."

"With chicken or quesillo?" he asked.

"Tonight, it's with chicken," she said.

That night, everyone was sleeping soundly when Esteban was awakened by a loud noise. Elina, also awake, told Esteban to stay close.

"Don't worry, Elina. I'm sure it's nothing," he said.

Before he could completely rise out of bed, several men kicked in the bedroom door. Elina screamed as the men repeatedly beat Esteban. The men then dragged Elina and Esteban to the living room where there was another group of men holding their sons at gunpoint. The men then paraded Esteban to the front of the room shouting and beating him. After a few moments, a man shot Esteban several times in the back of the head. Elina fell to her knees and wept. The boys were still too in shock to express any emotion of their own. One of the armed men then strode over to Fidel and held a pistol to his head. Elina crawled on her hands and knees to the man and begged him to spare her son's life. The man laughed, and then spit in Elena's face. Then, the leader of the group shouted some orders and the armed men left. Elina clutched her boys close to her and began weeping once again.

Fidel clenched his fists in anger and told Elina, "I will avenge Father!"

Elina immediately stopped crying and slapped Fidel hard. She shouted at him, "You will avenge nothing. Your father is gone. This is nothing you can do to bring my Esteban back." Fidel's face twisted in pain and he began to sob.

October, 2006
Yuma, Arizona

"Elina, you made it here in one piece."

"Not exactly, Fortuna. Several pieces of me were violated at the border."

"Was it that bad?" asked Fortuna.

"It doesn't matter," said Elina. "I did it for my boys."

"I'll help with everything, Elina," said Fortuna.

"First, I need a job and a place to stay," replied Elina.

"You can stay with us, of course, we're family. I can get you a job too. Do you mind housekeeping?"

"I will do anything to support my family, Fortuna. I will clean toilets, wash laundry, scrub floors—anything for my boys."

"I know someone that can give you a job. Don't worry. It is hard labor though and doesn't pay much."

"I will do so gladly."

"You're a good Mother, Elina, and your boys are beautiful too. You and Esteban did a fine job raising them. Now Esteban is gone, we must raise your sons as best we can. Do you miss him?"

"I talk to him every night before I go to bed."

"What do you talk about?"

"That we survived another day and are safe."

"God bless you, Elina."

"If we're lucky," replied Elina.

December, 2006

"Mom, are we really getting a home today?" asked Jose.

"Yes," replied Elina. "Now got get washed up. Fidel, Emillo—hurry up or you'll be late for work," commanded Elina.

"When are we going to get a car?" asked Emillo.

"I don't know," responded Elina. "You now have two choices; either use your legs or the bus"

"Yes, Mom," he replied.

"C'mon Jose; Mr. Jackson is expecting us soon."

"I'm ready, Mom. Let's go."

"Fidel, Emillo—you have our new address? Come right home after work."

"We will," responded Fidel."

"Okay, Jose, let's go."

Twenty minutes later, Elina and Jose arrived at the Rockport Apartments. Elina led Jose to the front office where a man was behind a desk watching TV. "Excuse me, Mr. Jackson. I'm here," announced Elina.

"About time," he snapped back. He then shot a stern look at Jose. "Is that yours?" he asked Elina.

"Yes, Mr. Jackson. This is Jose. He's my little man."

"Do you have my money?"

"Yes, sir," responded Elina.

"I get paid the first of the month. If you are late, I will throw you out."

"Yes, sir," responded Elina. "Here it is. You can count it if you like."

"Yes," he responded. "I don't know how well you people count."

Mr. Jackson then slowly got up from his chair and grabbed a key chain inside his drawer. He then tossed them to Elina and said once again, "The first of the month and that means every month."

"Yes, sir," said Elina. "I understand."

Mr. Jackson then made a sweeping hand gesture and returned to his television program.

"Let's go, Mom," Jose enthusiastically responded. "I can't wait to see my room."

Elina smiled back and led Jose to their new home.

Later that day, Fortuna's husband arrived at the apartment in a pickup truck filled with mismatched furniture. He called Elina on her cell to announce his arrival. Elina instructed Fidel and Emillo to go help their uncle bring in the items. Some of Elina's neighbors watched the move as they sat in the courtyard drinking beer.

"More Mexicans," one of the men complained.

"Just how many do you think they are going to squeeze into that tiny apartment?" the other responded.

"Who knows? I don't know how they can live like that."

"They're Mexicans, that's how. We would never do that." The other man spit and threw his empty beer can on the ground.

March, 2007

Elina work up at 4:30, the same time she did every morning. She entered the kitchen and put on a pot of coffee. This was one of the few down times of the day that she relished the opportunity to be alone. She poured herself a cup and went through the morning rituals. First, she said the Rosary. When that was completed, she pulled out the shoebox in the cupboard and placed it on the table. The shoebox was her only bank. For several months now Elina, Fidel, and Emillo had been depositing their pay into the box every Friday. Elina knew it was her family's life blood and she counted every morning. It was quite modest inside, but Elina wasn't worried. Elina only made $8/hour housekeeping and Fidel and Emillo made far less washing dishes at a local restaurant. "I'm so proud of my Fidel and Emillo," she said. "They work so hard and they're still just boys."

Then she placed the box back in the cupboard and resumed drinking her coffee. By six, she was dressed and had written her daily note for the boys before she left for work. She took the 172 bus to the Cranford Street transfer and then got on 12 bus, which delivered her close to her place of work. By 7:00, she arrived at the front stoop of the Thaker household. It was within an immaculately maintained community of large houses, expensive cars, and swimming pools. She brought in the paper, let the dogs out, and began fixing breakfast for the household. Mrs. Thaker was the first to greet Elina that morning. "Good morning, Elina."

"Good morning, ma'm," Elina responded.

"Elina," the woman continued. "I have been noticing spots on our dishes. I hate spots, Elina. I want you to start hand drying everything, Elina. Do you understand?"

"Yes, ma'm," Elina responded.

"Good," Mrs. Thaker continued. "And another thing. I need you to work this weekend. We are having visitors and I don't think I can manage alone."

"I can work this weekend," responded Elina.

"Good," said Mrs. Thaker. "Make sure you clean the house extra special before they arrive on Friday. I want to make a good impression."

"Yes, ma'm," responded Elina.

"You are the best," said Mrs. Thaker.

"Thank you, ma'm," Elina responded.

The remainder of the morning was spent getting the Thakers off to school and work. When they had all left, Elina went through the normal routine of cleaning the house, doing laundry, and watering the plants. After that, she then would have a couple of hours to rest before it was time to start fixing dinner for the Thakers. She usually spent it wondering what her boys were doing and if they were having a good day. By 7:00, she was back home to clean up after the boys and find out what they did that day. By 9:00, she was talking to Esteban and soon thereafter off to sleep.

March, 2008

"Mom?" asked Fidel.

"Yes, Fidel," she responded.

"I want to go back home!"

"This is your home now, Fidel," she said.

"I hate it here. We don't matter here!"

"What are you talking about?" she asked.

"We're invisible, Mom. If we left tomorrow, no one would know the difference."

"You think you are invisible, Fidel?"

"Yes. I know it for a fact. I feel it every day."

"You know what I feel every day, Fidel?"

"No."

"I feel you, Emillo, and little Jose. That's what I feel. You aren't invisible to me, Fidel. You aren't invisible to your brothers. You are very important to us. We need you, Fidel, every day. Do you understand?"

"No," replied Fidel.

"Just how do you think we would feel if we lost you?"

"I don't know," said Fidel.

"That's because you are still a boy, Fidel. When you grow into a man, you will understand exactly how we would feel."

"OK, Mom."

"Good. Now go get your brothers ready for church."

"Yes, Mom."

After Fidel left the room, Elina let out a soft cry and asked Esteban to help his son.

February, 2009

"Rice and beans again, Mom?" Emillo complained.

"Yes, Emillo," she responded. "I'm saving money for something very special."

"I like rice and beans, Mom," Jose said.

"That's my little man," responded Elina.

"He's not a little man, Mom," said Fidel. "He's a college boy. All he does is study. Emillo and me are men, we work."

Emillo then punched Jose in the arm. "Stop teasing Jose," Elina responded. "I'm proud of all my boys." Jose then punched Emillo back.

"What are you saving our money for, Mom?" asked Fidel.

Elina paused then said, "I want us to live in a house. I don't want you boys to all have to share one room together. I want a flower garden. Most of all, I want you boys to understand what hard work will get you in life."

"So far, it just gets us rice and beans," Emillo said. Jose punched Emillo in the arm once again.

June, 2009

"Fidel, you look so handsome in your suit," said Elina. "How does it feel on your Graduation Day?"

"Feels great, Mom. I'm a free man."

"You think so, Son?" asked Elina.

"Free from school, Mom. I hated it."

"That's OK, Fidel. It's not for everyone. However, you are definitely not free. Now, you must make your way in the world."

"Uncle Miquel said he would get me a job doing landscaping with him."

"Your Uncle Miquel is a good man, Fidel. Do what he tells you to do."

"I will, Mom."

"One more thing, Fidel, I want you to take this."

"I can't take your Rosary Beads, Mom. They mean so much to you."

"I don't need them anymore, Son. She lives in my heart now. Use them every day, Fidel. She listens and cares."

"OK, Mom; thanks."

"You don't have to move out you know if you don't want to."

"I'm not leaving until my mom gets her flower garden." Elina's eyes watered up and congratulated Fidel in becoming a man.

March, 2010

"Fortuna," Elina said. "I want a house more than anything."

"I know, Elina. How much money have you saved?"

"The boys and I have managed to put away $45,000."

"That's a lot of money, Elina. I'm so proud of you all."

"Every day I look in the classifieds to see what's available. I don't think we are quite there yet." Fortuna touched Elina's hand and asked, "How much do you need?"

"Oh, Fortuna. I would never ask you for money. You have already done so much for my family."

Fortuna responded, "I'm not keeping score, Elina. How much?" Elina's eyes watered up.

"I need about $20,000."

"Miquel and I have been saving for a while, Elina. We will give you the money."

"I can't take it," responded Elina.

"You can pay us back, Elina, but we don't expect you to if you can't." Elina hugged her sister and the two cried.

April, 2010

Elina saw the ad the previous week. It read "3 Bedroom Ranch, 1200 square feet, for sale by owner, $70,000 OBO". She knew the neighborhood and liked the posted picture. She called the listed number that Saturday to make arrangements for a showing. Upon arrival, she was greeted by an older woman that pretended to smile. "Hello, ma'm," said Elina. "I called earlier to see your home."

The older woman cleared her throat and asked Elina how she intended to pay for the home if interested. "I can pay in cash," she responded. The older woman then rolled her eyes and proceeded to give Elina a tour. The house needed some work. The carpet was badly stained in areas. The walls were in desperate need of a painting and many of the kitchen cabinets were either unhinged or completely missing a cover. Be that as it may, Elina fell in love with the home. She saw its potential and knew with a little help, it would be fine. She then asked the woman, "Can I see the backyard?" The woman then led Elina through the back sliding door. The backyard was cluttered empty pots, a broken swing set, and overgrown weeds. It did, however, face south and received plenty of sunlight.

Elina then told the woman, "I think I would like to make an offer."

"My listing price is $70,000," responded the woman.

"I understand, ma'm," said Elina. "But repairs are needed. Will you accept $61,000?"

The older woman scoffed at first. Then she asked, "You said cash, right?"

"Yes, ma'm. I will pay in cash."

"Fine," said the older woman. "You people are taking over the neighborhood anyway. So, what do I care?"

"Thank you, ma'm," responded Elina.

June, 2010

"Boys, get ready," said Elina. "Your Aunt Fortuna and cousins will be hear shortly."

"What are you fixing to eat, Mom?" asked Emillo.

"Chicken Empanadas," said Elina

"Smells great, Mom," he responded. "Can't wait."

What started out as a simple yard party with family, slowly grew into something more. Neighbors started filing in bringing food and warm wishes to welcome the new neighbors to the block. Fidel and his uncle, Miquel, arrived after a long days work to drink some beer and join the party. At the end of the evening, Elina's Jose told her to go to bed. He would clean up for her. Elina slowly undressed and made her way to bed. As she laid down, she reflected on her life in America. Her thoughts then turned towards Esteban. She had never really had the time to grieve properly for him. Tonight, however, she became overcome with emotion and cried uncontrollably calling out his name, saying how much she loved him and that the boys have a new house. After an hour, a great calm eventually took over her. She rose from bed and walked into the living room. There, she found her three sons had fallen asleep watching TV. Elina quietly turned off the television, gave a warm look towards her boys, and went back to bed.

JANE VS. JOHN

Jane was a working professional woman living in New York. She worked for a large advertising firm and was in charge of brand management. Her boyfriend, John was also a professional working in the banking industry. They had been going together for two years and living together the last four months. They enjoyed both a successful professional and social life. They loved each other very much and thought marriage might be imminent. So far, everything was going well. John learned how to share the bathroom and he took Jane's helpful instructions fairly well. Jane was very happy. She felt everything was just perfect.

"John," she asked. "Do you love me?" John knew the answer, but thought it was a loaded question. He knew if he said, "Yes" the next question would be "Why do you love me?" This was the question that bugged him. He couldn't explain why he loved Jane. He just did. What's more he knew this answer would be unsatisfactory to Jane. That said, he settled on responding, "What do you think, Jane?" Jane smiled and John was pleased he passed her test.

September

"Lisa," said Jane. "I'm late."
"How late?" asked Lisa.

"A week," said Jane.

"That's not too long."

"For many, yes. For me, no. I'm never late!"

"Just go to the pharmacy and get a kit."

"I did yesterday. I'm just too scared to look!"

"I think you'd better do it soon," said Lisa.

"Tell me something I don't know."

"I wouldn't worry too much about it. You're getting a little older. Maybe your body is just changing."

"Hope so."

"Does John know?"

"No and if you tell him, I'll be pissed."

"Don't worry."

That night after John fell asleep; Jane went to the bathroom and opened the box. It claimed the test was 99% accurate. Jane hoped for the best and followed the instructions. A few minutes later, she looked at the stick. It came back positive. "Fuck! Oh, shit, shit, fuck!" Jane took the evidence and stowed it safely away in the garbage. "I do not want to be pregnant. This sucks!" Jane then spent several hours in bed thinking before eventually falling asleep.

To be safe, the next day she made an appointment to see her doctor. After the examination, her doctor confirmed the news and congratulated her. Jane's facial expression, however, made it perfectly clear that she was not happy. The doctor picked up on this and reminded Jane she has options. That night, John noticed Jane was a bit fidgety and nervous. "Is everything OK?" he asked.

"What? Yes, everything is fine. I had a bad day at work."

"Do you want me to rub your shoulders?" he asked.

"Not right now, John. I don't think it would work anyway. Don't worry. I'll be fine by tomorrow."

"OK. Whatever you say."

The following day, Jane made arrangements to have lunch with her girlfriends for support. The luncheon proceeded as it normally did. They talked about work, dating, shopping. After placing their orders, Jane sighed and softly uttered, "I'm pregnant." "Jane, did you just say you're pregnant?" Jane covered her face with her hands and nodded.

"Does John know?" Jane shook her head. "Wow, that's inconvenient."

"Of course, it is," said Jane. "I can't be pregnant right now."

"I know it's unpleasant, but just get an abortion!"

"Obviously," said Jane.

"I think you should tell John though. It would be wrong to keep it from him."

"Of course," said Jane.

"He's an educated, contemporary guy. I'm sure he will support your decision."

"I know you're right," said Jane. "This still sucks though."

"Don't worry, Jane. Everyone will help you get through this"

That night John and Jane sat down to enjoy dinner together. They talked about their day at work, travel plans, and what to watch on TV that evening. They got up to put their dishes in the sink when Jane started crying. John, very confused, tried to console Jane and asked, "What is wrong?"

"John," she said. "I'm pregnant."

"Really?" said John. "How long?"

"A couple of weeks."

"Wow."

"Wow's right, John."

"That is totally awesome."

"What do you mean?"

"What do you mean by asking me what I mean? I think it's incredible."

"Oh, John, we're not close to being ready to have kids."

"I am, Jane. I'm quite ready to be a father."

"Fine. Well, I'm not ready to be a mother."

"What are you saying, Jane?"

"You're smart, John. Read between the lines."

"Oh, God, Jane, no, please no."

"I thought you would be more supportive!"

"I do support you, Jane. I love you very much. You know that."

"Then support me now and go along with it."

"No, Jane. I won't."

"Are you saying you are anti-abortion?"

"It's none of my business what other people do, Jane. That's their choice. It is my business, however, what we do. We are now responsible for a life. I take that responsibility very seriously."

"John, you don't know what you're saying."

"I know exactly what I am saying. I just said it and meant every word."

"What do you know about babies, John? If men got pregnant, abortion would be a sacrament.

"Thank you, Gloria Steinem. That's a real cute and clever statement but it doesn't make a whole lot of fucking sense. Women get pregnant. The die is cast, Jane. Get over it and grow up."

"I have rights, John. You know I have rights."

"You and your rights. Abortion and gun advocates are all the same about their rights. They both see red when questioned but don't question whether their rights are justified. You care more about your rights than the well-being of others."

"Roe vs. Wade says it all, John. Didn't you hear the news?"

"You mean the news said some jerk-off lawyer pulled out of his ass. Lawyers aren't paid to find justice. They are paid to win cases for their clients. Fuck the news, Jane."

"You have no say in the matter, John. It's my decision."

"If I believed in Immaculate Conception, I think I would agree with you. To the best of my knowledge, however, it doesn't exist. This isn't a woman's issue. It's an issue to be settled by both women and men. It's an adult issue. Fuck, Jane. If you're not ready to be a mother, I respect that. Just don't use euphemisms about your rights to hide the fact that you want to destroy our baby. Do you really expect me to defend that right when I don't think it should apply to us?"

"John, I don't want to see you right now."

"OK, I'll leave. I'll go to a hotel. Jane, promise me you won't do it. It would break my heart. Please don't do that to me. I love you so much. Please don't"

"I love you too John. Now, please just go."

John left several phone messages for Jane over the next couple of days that were left unreturned. Finally, Jane relented and called John back in the evening. "John."

"Jane, I've been so worried about you. Are you OK?"

"Yes, John, I'm fine."

"I'm sorry about our fight the other night, Jane. I know it's a very complicated issue. I should have been more understanding."

"You are right, John. It is complicated—especially for women. We really don't like getting abortions, John. Not at all."

"I'll shut up, Jane.

"No John, don't shut up. You were right. It is an adult issue between a woman and a man. I respect you, John, and your opinions. I always have."

"Then, you are not going to do it."

"No. I won't but I'm not ready to be a mother. I can sign custody over to you. In any event, I think its best we take a break for a while. I'll have papers sent to you right away."

"Jane, thank you from the bottom of my heart. Of course, I can help with medical expenses."

"That's nice of you John. But, I don't need or want your money. I have my own money."

"Of course," responded John. "Thanks again."

February

"Hi, Jane, I see you've filled out quite nicely!"

"Very funny, ha ha."

"Are you seeing John at all?"

"A little. I let him come to the last ultrasound. He was so attentive. When the technicians were doing their thing, he spoke up and said, 'Lego my Prego!' I love that. It was, I have to admit, a good icebreaker. He's so excited and proud, Lisa. Kind of inspires me."

"You're feeding it well obviously."

"That's enough."

"I'm just teasing you. You actually look beautiful."

"Much better."

"So, it is a boy. How does that make you feel?"

"I try not to feel too much, Lisa. I signed the papers and baby over to John. Besides, he has enough feelings for the both of us."

"John really is a good guy, Jane. I hope you get back together again someday."

"We'll see. Sometimes he texts me to say he still loves me. I believe him. I just don't want to be a mother right now."

April

Jane was not sleeping well at all. It was uncomfortable and she found herself needing to use the bathroom a lot during the night. "I can't wait to get this over with," she said. One morning at dawn, she opened her window to let in some fresh air. She was actually surprised and pleased to hear robins chirping. Jane had never paid much attention to birds. She saw them, but just never took the time to give them much thought. "This is a good way to start a day," she said to herself. That said, she decided she would start each morning listening to the robins sing.

A week later, she looked out her apartment window and noticed a nest with four small blue eggs. She spent her mornings and must of the weekend observing the mother robin attend to the eggs. Two weeks later, the eggs hatched. She noticed that the fledglings were naked and couldn't open their eyes. She also noticed that a robin with an orange breast was taking part in feeding the young birds. "Oh, my God," she said to herself. "I think it's the male." She became quite concerned with the robin family and found herself both crying and laughing while watching them interact.

Ten days later, two of the baby birds had left the next. "Please, God," she said to herself. "Take care of my little birds." Two days later, the other birds flew away. Jane cried uncontrollably.

May

"Any day now, Jane. You like you're ready to burst."

"I am, Lisa. I'm really glad you'll be with me during delivery. It means so much to me."

"Don't mention it. Is he still kicking? Let me touch your tummy. I want to see if I feel anything."

"Go ahead. Strangers do it on the street. You may as well do the same."

"He kicked. I felt it!"

"Yes, Lisa. He wants to come out and see you apparently."

"How are you feeling?"

"I'm a wreck. I don't know what to feel at this point. Goes in waves."

"Is John calling?"

"Every day. He's driving me nuts, but it's sweet."

A Week Later

"Push, Jane!"

"Fuck!"

"You're almost there, Jane. Just another big push!"

"Fuck!"

Suddenly, the room was filled with the sound of a screaming baby. Jane was completely exhausted and covered in sweat. The doctor smiled and said, "You did very well!"

The next morning, John visited Jane in her room. "Hi, Jane. Boy, you really look like shit. How do you feel?

"Like shit, less a hundred."

"You know I care, right?"

"I know John. I do. What did you name him?"

"Don't know quite yet, Jane; waiting for inspiration."

"You'll have to decide soon for his birth certificate."

"Maybe I'll be inspired soon."

"John?"

"Yes, Jane."

"Can I see him sometime?"

John felt an intense sense of emotion come over him and his face winced in pain. He looked away from Jane to fight away the tears. When he gained his composure, he found the strength to look at her in the eye, smile, and say, "Yes, Jane. We would both like to see you very much sometime."

IN THE NAME OF
THE FATHER

Gordon lived in Cedar Rapids, Iowa with his parents and two younger sisters. His dad was an insurance salesman and his mom was a homemaker. It was a deeply religious family that attended mass and church activities regularly. Gordon loved his church. He volunteered to be an altar boy and took the task very seriously. His parents, as well as the other parishioners that knew the family, were very proud of him and told him often. "I am going to be a priest someday, Mom," he would often tell his mother. She responded that would make her very proud and happy. When Gordon entered middle school, he was surprised to find girls and boys started taking a romantic interest in each other. Gordon and his friends never particularly cared for girls growing up. He wondered about the change in attitude and if he was next to fall victim. He hoped not. He wanted to be a priest first and knew they didn't take wives. When Gordon turned 15, he was still committed to resisting and did so quite easily. He did, however, start having feelings for men. He thought it was weird at first, and thankfully, he was largely able to block it from his mind altogether.

This ability to suppress his feelings remained strong as he progressed through high school. However, his friends asked him why he never dated anyone. Gordon, finally, gave into peer pressure and pursued a girl at the start of his junior year. He did like her as a good friend, so he didn't mind spending time with her. He then found his social life was more active and he enjoyed the camaraderie between other couples. Be that as it may, he still couldn't shake his attraction for males completely. He graduated high school and went to the University of Missouri. It was an exciting place; much more interesting than Cedar Rapids. He felt completely free to think for himself and he immersed himself in the college community. He still told his parents on the phone he wanted to someday be a priest, but now knowing in his heart it could never happen. He still loved God very much but now felt he could not remain celibate. Rather, he wanted to fall in love and help raise a Catholic family. He soon found a young woman he admired very much and they began seeing each other seriously. He really didn't feel a physical attraction to her but rather he loved her mind and companionship.

After three years of dating, Gordon decided to ask for her hand. She gladly accepted and they spent their senior year together happily engaged. Gordon was confident he did the right thing and was relieved that he had apparently talked himself out of becoming gay. He did sometimes get drunk and watch homosexual porn movies, but knew that was never a lifestyle he could adopt and accept. After the wedding in the summer, they moved to St. Louis where his wife was working in a human resources department and Gordon found work for a popular retailer. They didn't make a lot of money, but were content with their lifestyle and made the most of it by participating incommunity and church activities.

Gordon liked his job very much and worked hard every day. He was particularly drawn to a co-worker names Thomas and they soon began going out for drinks after work. The more time Gordon spent with Thomas, the harder he found it to control his urges. On the other hand, spending time with Thomas made him feel more alive than he did his whole life. Gordon was torn. He spent evenings praying in earnest. "Please, God, I beg you to fix me," he cried. Gordon's prayers were not fulfilled and he became more deeply involved with Thomas. Thomas, the whole while, knew Gordon's feelings and was welcoming all the advances. Thomas had been openly gay since high school, and understood what Gordon was going through. He remained patient, but it was getting harder. After one night of hard drinking, Thomas kissed Gordon. Gordon wanted to resist but couldn't.

Six month later, Gordon sat down with his wife. "Julie, I have something very serious to tell you." Julie's attention perked up immediately and she said, "Oh!"

"Julie, there is no good way to put this. I'm gay."

"What? No you're not!"

"I am. I'm so sorry."

"Gordon," she responded. "For how long?"

"Since I was a boy. I fought it as hard as I could, but can't anymore."

"How could you do this to me?" she screamed.

"I'm so sorry, Julie. I never wanted to hurt you!"

Two months later, they were divorced. Gordon's parents were devastated, but Gordon was happier than he'd ever been. He experienced true love with Thomas and that's all that mattered to him. Eventually, he started to learn to accept his lifestyle and lead a good life. As his confidence grew, he found his faith also became even stronger. Instead of praying, "God, please fix me;" he prayed, "God, thank you for letting me feel love." Influenced by Thomas' urging, Gordon decided to come out in front of his family. "Fine, I'll just do it," he told him. That Friday, he took off work to drive back to Iowa. He arrived that evening and was stressed. His mother greeted him with open arms. "Gordy, welcome home!"

"It is good to be home, Mom. Thanks." His sisters were next to greeting him. They gave him a big hug and kiss on the cheek each. His father entered the room, shook his hand firmly, and they all knelt down to thank God for his safe return home. In the morning, Gordon's mother was fixing him breakfast. "Smells good, Mom. Sausage, eggs, toast, the staples of the Midwest." After finishing his breakfast, Gordon requested the family gather around. After a few minutes, the entire family assembled at the table. "Okay, Gordon," said his father. "What's the news?" At first Gordon opened his mouth, but found he couldn't manage to generate any sound. He then cleared his throat and said, "I've found true love." His mother was very pleased and clapped her hands. "That's great, Son. What's her name?" asked his dad.

Gordon once again found it difficult to speak. He then let out a deep breath and said, "His name is Thomas!"

"I'm not sure I follow you, Gordy," said his mother.

"Mom," he responded. "I'm gay."

The silence lasted for a good 30 seconds until Gordon's father broke by screaming, "What are you saying?"

"I'll say it again. I'm gay!"

Gordon's sisters looked at him in disgust. His mother wept and his father pounded the table. "You're an abomination," he screamed. Gordon remained calm by thinking of Thomas.

"Dad, maybe I am an abomination. Who knows; but it's not my choice. I didn't choose to be this way."

"We must pray," Gordon's mom yelled.

"Mom, I pray every night. I used to cry and ask to be fixed. Now, I pray to give thanks for having someone."

"God hates homosexuals!" his father shouted. "I didn't ever think you can pray to God as one of those."

"I don't think so, Dad. What's more, I love God very much. I will pray whenever I feel like it."

"Get out of my sight!" his father screamed. "Don't ever come back here."

"But, Dad, I love you and my family. I want to be part of your life."

"We will never be part of your sick life. Get out now."

Gordon's mother said nothing and wept in her hands. Gordon fought very bravely to fight back his own tears. By the time he reached the car, however, he gave in and fell to the ground in pain. The ride home was awful. The people he'd known his whole life, completely abandoned him. He called Thomas often when he had to pull over and take a break. By the time he reached home, he had cried himself dry and just wanted a drink and a good night's rest. He prayed to God that night thanking him once again for allowing him to experience Thomas.

In the months that followed, Gordon started spending more and more time attending services. He felt it filled the void left by his family. He was particularly hurt by his father's assertion that God hates homosexuals. Father Robert noticed Gordon's despair and approached him one day after service. "I see you here a lot. What's going on? Is anything troubling you?"

"Yes; a lot is troubling me."

"Maybe we could talk, I can help if you let me."

"I don't think I can talk to you about my situation."

"But that's what I'm here for. My calling is to look after my flock. Tell you what. Why don't we have dinner some night this week? You might start to feel a whole lot better."

Gordon agreed but wasn't sure if he could broach the subject with a priest. Thursday night came, and Gordon arrived at the priest's home on time. First, they shared a glass of wine discussing upcoming events and eventually settled in for a pasta dinner. After dinner, Father Robert asked Gordon if he felt he can talk to him now. "I'm quite certain I can't," he responded. "But, I will anyway."

"Good," said Father Robert. "Out with it, Son."

"My father and family have disowned me. My only solace is praying to God."

"You mean the Father," the priest said.

"Yes. The big Father," replied Gordon.

"Why did they disown you?"

"I'll tell you, but you won't like it. I can't afford to be thrown out of the parish."

"Throw you out. I wouldn't presume I had the right to do such a thing."

"OK. They disowned me because I'm gay." Father Robert took a sip of wine and assured Gordon he certainly wouldn't throw him out of church for something like that. "But, it's your church," replied Gordon. "I thought you and Rome had some sort of understanding."

Father Robert took another sip of wine. "It's not my church. It's not Rome's church. It's Christ's church, Son. Who am I to decide who can and cannot talk to Him in His house?"

"My father says God hates homosexuals."

"Do you think God is hate, Son?"

"No. I think God is love. At least that's what I believe."

"I think I agree with you."

"Do you hate me because I'm gay?"

"Son, do you know what the Gospel says about human sexuality?"

"No. I don't," said Gordon.

"Nothing, I don't hate you and I don't believe the Father hates his son Gordon either. I think He loves you very much. That's what I think, Son."

Gordon became overwhelmed with emotion and cried out, "I'm so sorry."

Father Robert touched Gordon on the shoulder. "You have nothing to be sorry about. Are you saying you're sorry for being yourself?"

"Yes. That's exactly what I'm saying. I never wanted to be gay. I just wanted to be loved."

"Are you loved by someone?"

Gordon wiped the tears away from his eyes with his sleeve and sniffled, "Yes. I am very much so I feel it every day."

"Then, thank God for your gifts."

"I do every night."

"Then, I can see you are a member of my flock worth receiving Christ's way of help and salvation. Have a sip of wine. He shed it for you."

THE LOTTERY

Tyrus and Sebastian grew up next door neighbors on Powell Street in Detroit. It was an impoverished neighborhood with abandoned cars, boarded up houses, and empty lots filled with trash. Be that as it may, they both managed to lead a happy childhood together. When they were 13, Tyrus told Sebastian he thought of him and his little brother and would always look out for him. This made Sebastian feel good. He always looked up to Tyrus—the stronger and more popular of the two.

When they entered Martin Luther King High School, they found the experience quite overwhelming. "This place is rough," Tyrus told Sebastian. "We got to watch each other's backs." Sebastian agreed although he understood that it would be Tyrus watching his back. Despite the hostile environment, Sebastian loved going to school and learning. Tyrus often teased Sebastian accusing him of being white for being so studious. This didn't bother Sebastian so long as he knew he had a good friend and protector. Tyrus, on the other hand, had always hated attending class. He found he got much more attention and satisfaction when he did well in sports. They both dedicated their freshman year to their interests and tried to capitalize on their individual talents. Tyrus excelled on the playing field, whereas Sebastian excelled in the classroom. This split in passions led both boys to spend fewer time together. By the end of the second quarter, the two really didn't spend much time together at all. Tyrus had his jock friends. Sebastian, on the other hand, kind of blended into the scene and didn't have many friends at all. Be that as it may, they both supported each other when they had a moment in the hallway and chance encounters on the weekends.

By sophomore year, Tyrus had established themselves as a premier athlete and Sebastian as a premier student. That said, the faculty gave both of them a lot of attention in their perspective areas.

Mr. Johnson, the Varsity football coach, talked with Tyrus often and invited him to work out with the Juniors and Seniors. "Think you have what it takes to make it, Tyrus?" he asked.

Tyrus confidently responded, "I will do whatever it takes, Coach."

"Good," Mr. Johnson said. "Don't worry about grades. The team needs you!"

"Yes, Sir," responded Tyrus.

Regarding Sebastian, the Honors English teacher, Mr. Williams, took a very strong interest in him. "You're a very gifted writer, Son," he said. "I want to help you develop your natural gift." This pleased Sebastian. He looked up to Mr. Williams and saw him as friend.

The next weekend, Tyrus and Sebastian bumped into each other on the corner. "Hey, Sebastian. How's my little smart friend doing?"

Sebastian chuckled and said, "Fine. How's my dumb jock friend doing?"

Tyrus grinned, "I'm going great. Coach Johnson says I have plenty of talent to make it to the next level."

Sebastian smiled, "Mr. Williams said the same thing about me!"

"Mr. Williams is a cracker," responded Tyras. Sebastian laughed; then said, "He's actually a pretty cool guy."

"Whatever you say," said Tyrus.

"Tyrus," said Sebastian. "I want to go to Harvard."

"I bet you would fit in fine with all those rich while folk," said Tyrus.

"Where do you want to go?" asked Sebastian.

"Me? I'm a Michigan man. Coach Johnson knows people there and says I can get looked at."

"That would be awesome, Tyras. Michigan is a really good school."

"I don't give a damn about school, Sebastian. I'm a football player. I'll put up with the school stuff until I make it to the Pros"

"I know you can do it, Tyras. Go for it!"

"I aim to little brother," responded Tyrus.

That summer, Tyrus started hanging out with the Varsity football players regularly. They lifted weights, went to parties, and chased girls. Sebastian spent the summer working on his writing, preparing for the ACT's, and working to save money for college. By the time junior year was well under way, both were really hitting their stride. Tyrus was starting at Halfback and Sebastian was placing out of college introductory courses.

Mr. Williams was following Sebastian's progress closely. He approached him in the hall one day. "You're doing fine work, Son. I'm really proud of you. Have you started thinking about schools yet?"

"Yes, Mr. Williams. I'm just thinking of one school!"

"Which on is that school?" asked Mr. Williams.

"Harvard," responded Sebastian.

Mr. Williams was pleased. "I think it's great you are setting your sights high, Son. You are bound by nothing. Still, I think it would be smart to apply to more than just one school."

"It has to be Harvard, Mr. Williams. I want to be a Harvard man."

"Son," said Mr. Williams. "I do believe you could be just about any man you choose to become."

"Thanks," said Sebastian. "I know you believe in me. It means a lot."

"I understand, Sebastian, it means a lot to an old teacher like me to hear you say that! C'mon Son, let me buy you a pop."

"Okay," said Sebastian. "Thanks."

By the end of the fall, Tyrus had broken the school record for most yards rushed in a season. Sebastian had just finished the ACT's and was confident he performed well. Tyrus was in his glory. He had a very active social life and was being groomedby college football programs across the Midwest.

In early January, Sebastian received the results of his ACT exam. "This is it," he said. "Tyrus is King of the world right now. This is my chance to join him and get into Harvard." He ripped open the envelope and read a score of 23. "23. Is that it?" he said. "I thought I did better." The next day at school, he confided as much to Mr. Williams.

"Mr. Williams," he said. "I only got a 23 on my ACT!"

"23 is a very good score, Sebastian. Congratulations."

"I don't know if it is good enough to get into Harvard though."

"Do you think you are really defined by a score on one test? Do you think you are defined by what school you go to? I think you are defined by your quality of work and character. That's what I think, Son."

"I just have to get into Harvard, Mr. Williams. If I don't, I just don't know what I'll do."

Mr. Williams paused for a moment; then said, "You could still get into Harvard, Sebastian. You've done really good work while here. I want to you to do me a big favor though. I want you to apply to another school or two. Can you do that for me, Son? It would mean a lot to me."

"Which one?" asked Sebastian.

"How about Michigan State? That's where I went to school, Sebastian. I would even be willing to give you a personal campus tour."

"Well, it is a Big Ten school. They're all good."

"Yes, Son, they are. Keep this in mind though. It really doesn't matter what school you go to. It's what you put into it. That's how life works, Son, not just school. It applied to students. It applies to everyone like lawyers, carpenters, and even old teachers like me."

"I know you are a great teacher, Mr. Williams. I respect and admire you."

"Thank you, Son. I respect and admire you as well."

"OK, Mr. Williams. I'll apply but I want to go to Harvard."

"Go for it, Son," said Mr. Williams.

Sebastian retook the ACT several more times but couldn't improve upon his score. By the fall of his senior year, he relented and accepted his score. Soon thereafter, he applied to Harvard and Michigan State. Tyrus was having another stellar season on the field. It was well ahead of his previous season's mark in yardage. In the final regular season game of the year, however, tragedy struck. He took the hand-off and hit the line hard. The opposing defensive end, however, hit him even harder knocking him to the ground. Tyrus laid there paralyzed, unable to move. The paramedics had to eventually move him off the field and deliver him to a local emergency room. The operation lasted six hours.

The next day, Tyrus was greeted by the doctor. He was extremely sore and somewhat dazed. "You're a very lucky young man," the doctor said. "You could have been paralyzed. Your back was broken in two vertebrae."

"Thanks," said Tyrus. "If I couldn't play ball, I don't know what I would do."

The doctor gave Tyrus a very serious look and said, "You're not paralyzed, but you could be if you continue playing football and re-injure your back. I'm noting it on your file. Sorry, Son."

"I could get a second opinion," responded Tyrus.

"No doctor is going to let you play at any level. Sorry."

By February, things were progressing nicely for the Seniors. They knew they were close to graduation and were using every opportunity to take advantage of their position. Tyrus as devastated at first by his twist of fate. On the other hand, he had gained a lot of respect and admiration in the local community and remained extremely popular and well-liked. Sebastian

had received his response letter from Michigan State first. He really didn't
have must interest in attending, so he stuffed it in his backpack and soon
forgot about it. When the letter from Harvard arrived, he was overcome
with anxiety. He couldn't open it. Rather, he held it next to his bedside
lamp to see if he could make out the writing against the light. After a few
days, however, he found the courage to look inside. His hand shook as he
unfolded the page. The then began reading.

> Dear Applicant,
>
> We appreciate your interest and are impressed with your
> background.
>
> However, we regret to inform you that . . . .

Sebastian dropped the letter and began to cry.

A few weeks later, he ran into Tyras on the corner. "Hey Sebastian,
what's up?"

"Not good," said Sebastian. "I didn't get into Harvard."

"Hah," yelled Tyrus. "Now you're just like the rest of us. Welcome
back, my nigga."

"It sucks," admitted Sebastian.

"Don't worry about a thing. I'll introduce you to my friends. We'll have
a great time."

"Really," asked Sebastian.

"Sure, my little brother. Welcome back." In the weeks that followed,
Sebastian began hanging out with Tyrus more and more. They had fun
drinking beer, smoking pot, and skipping school. It was just like the old
days for Sebastian. He had his friend Tyrus back and he didn't care about
Harvard any more.

The next Friday, Tyrus told Sebastian to come to a party in the
neighborhood. It was being held by some young men a few years older than

Tyrus. Tyrus met them through his football days when they came to the game to watch him play. It made Tyrus feel good to be accepted by adults and he made the most of the opportunity. Sebastian was very excited to be invited and was grateful his friend Tyrus was helping him. When Sebastian arrived, the party was in full swing. Drinks, drugs and music were flowing. Sebastian was intimidated, but strove to make a good impression in front of Tyrus. When he came across his friend, he noticed Tyrus was already quite drunk and slurring his words badly. "Where you been, my nigga," said Tyrus. "The party started early today."

"I can see that," said Sebastian. "Thanks for inviting me."

"No problem, my little brother. Let me introduce you around."

Tyrus led Sebastian to a group of young men. He stumbled and laughed to himself. Sebastian felt extremely uncomfortable and out of place. After approaching, the young men looked over Sebastian and let it be known that they did not approve. "No," said Tyrus. "This is my little brother, Sebastian. He's with me."

"Sebastian," said one of the men. "What kind of fucked up name is that?"

Sebastian then spoke up, "Tyrus, I think I should go."

"I think you should go too, nigga," said one of the other men. "Before you get hurt."

"No," said Tyrus. "He's with me." He then laughed and stumbled in his place once more. One of the men then pushed Sebastian hard. He then said, "He can stay, but first he has to fight me."

Tyrus laughed and told Sebastian, "Go ahead Sebastian, don't take his shit!"

Sebastian stood there unable to think or move. The same man pushed him even harder once again. He then said, "I think this asshole will take my shit. I don't like him."

The other men started laughing and taunting Sebastian as well. Shortly thereafter, they grabbed Sebastian into the front yard. Sebastian felt completely helpless and vulnerable. The men surrounded Sebastian in a circle and started taking turns punching him. Sebastian eventually doubled over in pain and fell to the ground.

"Tyrus," said one of the men. "You are either with us or your asshole little brother. What will it be?"

Tyrus didn't bother to even pause. "Fuck it," Tyrus said. "Let's get a drink and slapped some of his friends on the back and stumbled back inside.

The following Monday, Sebastian returned to school. He was quite bruised and depressed. After school, he paid a visit to Mr. Williams. "There you are Sebastian. I've missed you. What happened to your face?"

"I would rather not talk about it," said Sebastian.

Mr. Williams paused a moment. "That's fine, Son. We don't have to."

"Mr. Williams, I didn't get into Harvard."

"Too bad, Son. I know how much it meant to you. In my view, it meant too much."

"What do you mean?" asked Sebastian.

"Son, I've been teaching in this community since 1976 and I've seen a lot of stuff."

"What kind of stuff?" asked Sebastian.

"I've seen a lot of lottery losers," said Mr. Williams.

"Not sure I follow," said Sebastian.

Mr. Williams removed his glasses. "This is a rough neighborhood. People think the only way to escape is by being the hero. Every day it's the bottom of the 9th, full count, bases loaded, and down by three runs. Every day the batter is still swinging for the fences trying to hit the grand slam. For most, the grand slam is making it in sports or music. For you, it was Harvard. Most strike out. I don't want to see you strike out, Son. I want to see you advance the runners and keep the inning alive. There is nothing wrong with a single or even a walk, Son. Am I getting through to you?"

"I think so," said Sebastian.

"Good, so you didn't get into Harvard. Did you get into Michigan State?

"Not sure," replied Sebastian. "Never opened the letter."

"Do you have it with you?" asked Mr. Williams.

Sebastian reached inside his backpack and pulled out the crinkled letter. He handed it to Mr. Williams and asked him to read it for him. Mr. Williams put his glasses back on and opened the letter. Sebastian hung his head to await the news. After a few minutes, Sebastian asked Mr. Williams what it said. Mr. Williams looked Sebastian in the eye and replied, "It says you are going to Michigan State. How does that make you feel, Son?"

"I'm not sure. Don't know exactly what to feel, Mr. Williams."

"Call me by my first name, Sebastian. It's Sean."

"OK, Sean. Thanks for everything. I'm not sure what is going to happen to me."

"Follow your heart, Son. You'll do fine. C'mon, let me buy you a pop."

IRON AND WINE

Dan loved being a grandfather. He was part of the Nez Perce tribe in Idaho. He learned much from his own grandfather when he was a child and relished the opportunity to impart his wisdom onto his grandson also named Daniel. He would take his grandson to daily walks and show him good and bad within nature. The Grandson thought it was a bit much. He much rather preferred playing video games. Be that as it may, Daniel adored his grandfather and he did his best to abide by his lessons. Dan loved the grey wolf. His own grandfather taught him wolves help create balance in nature and are a very good thing. When Dan was a boy, his grandfather brought him to a spot in the woods at night and they listened for the wolves cry. Both Dan and his grandfather smiled at the sound and were very pleased. Many years later, Dan contemplated bringing his grandson, Daniel, to the same spot to hear the wolves cry. Wolves, however, were becoming more rare. Ranchers nearby shot them to protect their cattle.

One night, Dan decided the time had come and took his grandson to the same spot in the woods. Dan was very excited as he remembered the moment he shared with his grandfather 63 years ago. After some effort, they managed to arrive. Dan was very pleased and told Daniel he was something very important to show him. "Okay, Grandpa. Whatever you say." One hour passed and there was no sound. Daniel became restless and pulled out his Walkman. Another hour passed, still no sound. Daniel told him grandfather he was cold and wanted to go home.

"Just a little longer, Daniel. Give it a chance. I promise you'll like it."

"Okay, Grandpa."

Dan was growing nervous and looked at his watch often. By 10 p.m., still no sound. "Grandpa, can we please go? I'm tired." Dan hung his head and wept. "Why are you crying, Grandpa?" asked Daniel.

Two years later, Daniel was living in Siskiyou County in Northern California with his mother. The previous year was difficult. Daniel lost his grandfather. Then, his father was killed by a drunk driver a month later. Daniel's mother had become a Christian to help ease the pain. She decided it best to leave the reservation in Idaho and raise her son in California. Daniel loved living in Northern California. It was very beautiful and he often took long walks and thought of his grandfather.

"Mom," said Daniel. "You're a Christian but you never go to church."

"The world is my church, Daniel. I see good and evil every day."

"Do you want me to be a Christian, Mom? I will if you want me to."

"That is completely up to you, Daniel. This is my own spiritual journey, Daniel. It's very personal to me. I can't and won't make you take it with me. I want you to choose and take your own journey, Daniel. You will get a lot more out of it."

"I like nature, Mom. It reminds me of Grandpa."

"That is perfectly fine with me, Daniel."

Daniel was an exceptional student. He excelled in both math and science. His mother was very encouraging and praised him often. "Mom, can I go to college?"

"Of course, you can, Daniel. That would make me very proud."

"Part of me thinks I should stay and take care of you."

"No Daniel. It would hurt me very badly if you did that. We left the reservation, Daniel. I want my son to experience and participate in the world. It means a lot to me, Daniel."

"Okay, Mom. I'll listen."

The falling year, Daniel received a full tuition scholarship to San Diego State. They drove down together at the end of the summer to deliver Daniel to college. The drive took two days and Daniel did most of the talking. His mother was quiet and stoic. They eventually reached the dormitory and unloaded the car. Suddenly, Daniel realized that he was about to lose his mother. "Mom?"

"Yes, Daniel."

"Will you stay the night? I want you to be here tomorrow morning."

"Of course, I will, Daniel. I'll stay at a motel. You can stay here in the dorm.

We can have breakfast together in the morning, but I will have to leave after that."

"Thanks, Mom."

The next morning Daniel and his mother ate breakfast together at a nearby café. "Daniel?"

"Yes, Mom."

"You are about to start your journey through life. There are many pitfalls. I can't always be here for you anymore. But I will always love you."

"Okay, Mom."

"Remember where you came from and spread your wings. I want to see you fly someday, Daniel."

"Yes, Mom."

Daniel struggled at first and called his mother often. She has always been supportive and told Daniel how proud she was of him. Daniel's one escape from the pressure of being on his own was his studies. It helped him focus his thoughts and forget about his stress. He also made a point to go for walks in the park every morning. He liked to watch his environment wake up and start the day anew and rested. He got very good grades his first year. This pleased his mother very much. When she drove down to pick him up in the spring, she expressed as much. "I'm so proud of you, Daniel. You did exceptionally well your first year away. Many don't."

"Thanks, Mom. I just remembered what you told me. It really helped a lot."

"Good. The first year away is the hardest. It will get easier; you'll see."

"Okay, Mom. I believe you."

The start of his sophomore year went well. He started feeling more confident about his surroundings and strove to navigate it better. His social life improved through a student political group. Their main focus was environmental issues. They distributed information around campus and organized small but passionate rallies. He called and told his mother often of the state of the world and how much it bothered him. "I'm very pleased, Daniel, and your grandfather would be too.

The start of his junior year he decided he wanted to major in Biology. He loved the environment very much and wanted to understand how it managed to work. He diligently worked on his studies, but went even further by investing in his own personal books and journals, which he read in his spare time. That summer, he stayed in San Diego and worked for an environmental protection group. Daniel loved it. He appreciated being around people that felt just as passionately about the environment as he did.

At the end of his senior year, his mother drove down for graduation. She was beaming and Daniel noticed as much. "Mom?"

"Yes, Daniel."

"I've been thinking lately."

"Oh? About what?"

"What happened to our people?"

"Go on, Daniel."

"Mom, the Jewish people have a name for what happened to them. The Holocaust. Do we have a name, Mom, for what happened to us? I want to know!"

"If there was a name, I wouldn't tell it to you."

"Mom, our people have lived in darkness a long time. It hurts me. You know what I think now?"

"What, Daniel."

"I think we are the Chosen People. I think God chose for us to suffer the most, but He wants us to honor Him anyway. Do you think we are the Chosen People, Mom?"

"I don't know, Daniel. It's not really all that important to me. But know this, Daniel. Your mother does not live in darkness and I don't want my son to either. Okay, Daniel? I want my son to live in the light and his spirit to soar. That's what I want, Daniel."

"Mom, I love earth so much. I want to dedicate my life and energy to fight for it every day."

"I believe you can, Daniel. I believe you are ready to fly."

Daniel stayed in San Diego and got a job with the California Wolf Center. There was speculation that the grey wolf was going to migrate west to Northern California to seek a more hospitable environment. In anticipation, the organization Defenders of Wildlife had petitioned the federal government to set aside land to be used for wolf habitat. Daniel was extremely motivated. Many California residents were already upset by protection regulation on behalf of owls and fish. They were determined to stand their ground and keep the wolves out of California. Daniel thought different. He worked tirelessly of the wolves behalf over the next several years. The resistance in Siskiyou County where Daniel's mother still lived was particularly intense. That said, Daniel and his girlfriend decided to move north and start a grass roots group based in the county. The wolves began migrating on their own, and Daniel's group fought for many years on their behalf. Eventually, he retired from organizing and sought to spend more time with the grandchildren. Daniel loved being a grandfather. He felt spending time with them made him feel younger and stronger. Daniel's oldest daughter had a son, which she named Daniel, but his grandfather called him Danny. Danny looked up to his grandfather and he loved going for walks with him. Daniel pointed out all the things in the ecosystem and Danny paid close attention. One weekend, Daniel took his grandson camping. They went for walks, talked and laughed. On the last night of the trip, Daniel was sitting by the campfire telling him stories about his own grandfather. Danny was filled with pride and recognized he was part of a great past. It was at that moment that they were interrupted by the sounds of a wolf howling. Daniel looked at his grandson and then looked up at the sky. "Why are you crying, Grandpa?" asked Danny.